Hugh Doran

PHOTOGRAPHER

THE IRISH ARCHITECTURAL ARCHIVE

45 Merrion Square, Dublin 2

HUGH DORAN — PHOTOGRAPHER
First published in 2007 by
The Irish Architectural Archive, 45 Merrion Square, Dublin 2.

Designed by: David Hayes.

Printed by: Vision Print.

Photographic reproduction: Richard Dann and Photolabs.

ISBN 978-0-9515536-3-3

FRONT COVER: *Leixlip Castle, Co. Kildare, bedroom.*

HUGH DORAN (1926 - 2004) was an amateur photographer of extraordinary talent. A native of Dublin and a printer by profession who spent his working life in Arthur Guinness & Co., Hugh's interest in photography began as a teenager. He joined the Photographic Society of Ireland in 1949 and was from the mid-1950s a regular contributor to – and medal winner at – the Society's exhibitions. His photographs were also included in exhibitions in Berlin, Bordeaux, Bermuda, San Sebastian and Vienna.

Hugh's camera focused on a variety of subjects from portrait to landscape, but two themes stand out – architecture and his native city. Hugh's interest in architecture was long-standing. He travelled extensively in Ireland and abroad, compiling albums of these trips which focused very much on the buildings he had visited. His eye for detail was precise and his composition outstanding. In 1959 Desmond Guinness asked Hugh to photograph Irish town and country houses – specifically those with curved wings – for an Irish Georgian Society exhibition. A new interest was sparked. Over the succeeding decades Hugh photographed many of the grandest of Ireland's houses, charming owners to allow him to capture not only the stately exteriors but also the fully furnished interiors. These photographs have gone on to illustrate and enhance numerous publications on the Irish country house.

Hugh's Dublin photographs are perhaps more personal. They capture a Dublin now vanished, a city free of cars and laced with shadow, an old city, faded certainly and derelict in places yet still full of life. Portraiture and architectural photography combine in images which reveal as much of the personality of the city as its built fabric.

Hugh was an active member of at least fourteen different organisations and societies. He was also, from 1991 until just before his death, a volunteer with the Irish Architectural Archive. He ran the Archive's reading room every Wednesday, freely dispensing his wealth of knowledge – architectural, photographic and beyond – to the Archive's readers and researchers. Consistently dapper and universally courteous, Hugh was a true gentleman. He is sadly missed and fondly recalled by many of those who use the Archive and most especially by all who work there.

In accordance with his wishes, Hugh's widow Kitty transferred his photographs to the Irish Architectural Archive in 2005. The Hugh Doran Collection is without question one of the single most important acquisitions of photographs in the Archive's thirty-year history. This publication, made possible through the support of John Sisk & Son Ltd and the Department of Arts, Sport & Tourism, merely skims the surface of the collection. Hopefully however it provides a flavour of its contents as well as an indication of its quality.

Michael Webb
Chairman
Irish Architectural Archive
June 2007

HUGH DORAN — AN APPRECIATION

MARIGA AND I FIRST MET Hugh Doran in 1958 when we founded the Irish Georgian Society (IGS). He worked in the Guinness Brewery printing works, where the labels for every bottle of stout for every pub in Ireland were printed. The publican was issued with a pot of glue and a brush and his name, address and the date of the brew (backwards) were on the labels. *The Harp*, a magazine for brewery employees, was also printed here as well as the programmes for plays and concerts that took place in the Rupert Guinness Hall.

The first exhibition arranged by the IGS on Irish architecture was specially photographed by Hugh and opened on the 14th July 1959 in the Little Theatre of Brown Thomas. To give it a theme we called it 'A Study in Curves' as it was evident that curved sweeps were a feature common to many Irish buildings in both town and country. In Dublin there are Charlemont House and Powerscourt House, as a start, and in the country Castletown (Conolly) and Florence Court, Co. Fermanagh where the curves are at the back of the house. Lord Enniskillen was hard of hearing, and was totally convinced that Hugh was me, when Mariga drove him up there. 'A Study in Curves', like all the Brown Thomas exhibitions, was well covered in the newspapers and justifiably so; it also provided a temporary city base to distribute IGS literature and membership forms.

Leixlip was far from a haven of warmth and comfort when we moved in, and Hugh was one of the first friends brave enough to stay here in 1953 when we bought the castle - there was neither electricity nor central heating for what seemed like eternity. He came on the Society's first 'foreign' tour in 1960 to Edinburgh and the wonderful houses that surround it. Hugh carried a very weighty tripod and made a miraculous record of all we saw, working at great speed and overcoming the practical difficulties that he faced. Both his Scottish prints and negatives are in the Irish Architectural Archive along with the rest of his work, mainly of course Irish. It is hard to believe that the Edinburgh tour was nearly fifty years ago. Just you try booking a bus-load of Irish into a central hostelry because it charged just two guineas a night, only to discover it was a temperance hotel!

Desmond Guinness

Desmond Guinness
Leixlip
June 2007

Guinness Power Station from Watling Street, Dublin.

1954

ORIGINAL TITLE: 'POWER'.

EXHIBITED:
Photographic Society of Ireland, 1955.
Internationale Foto und Verbandsausstellung, Berlin, 1955.
Salón Internacional de Fotografía de Vitoria, 1955.
VIIe Salon International d'Art Photographique, Photo-Club de Bordeaux, 1956.
20 years of Pictorial Photography, Photographic Society of Ireland, 1959.

Pont Valentré, Cahors, France.

1953

ORIGINAL TITLE: 'PONT VALENTRÉ'.

EXHIBITED:
Photographic Society of Ireland, 1958.

Lambay Castle, Co. Dublin.

1963

ORIGINAL TITLE: 'STUDY OF A STUDY'.

EXHIBITED:
Photographic Society of Ireland, 1964.
Cork Photographic Exhibition, 1965.

Muckross Friary, Co. Kerry.

1952

ORIGINAL TITLE: 'CLOISTER'.

EXHIBITED:
Photographic Society of Ireland, 1953.
An Óige Exhibition, An Tóstal, 1957.

Dublin Airport, Collinstown, Co. Dublin.

1954

Liberty Hall, Dublin.
1965

St. Patrick's Church, Lower Glanmire Road, Cork.
1965

Meknes, Morocco.

1965

ORIGINAL TITLE: 'THE FLOWING TIDE'.

EXHIBITED:
International Cork Photographic Exhibition, 1966.

Cathedral Church of St. Mary and St. Anne, Cathedral Road, Cork.

1952

EXHIBITED:
Photographic Society of Ireland, 1953.
An Óige Exhibition, An Tóstal, 1957.

St. Mary's Chapel of Ease (the Black Church), St. Mary's Place, Dublin.
1962

Christ Church Cathedral, Dublin, West Front.
1955

Guinness Trust Flats, Kevin Street, Dublin.

1960

ORIGINAL TITLE: 'MONDAY MORNING'.

EXHIBITED:
Photographic Society of Ireland, 1961.

Heuston Station, Dublin.
1950

John's Lane, Dublin.

1955

ORIGINAL TITLE: 'SUNDAY MORNING'.

EXHIBITED:
Photographic Society of Ireland, 1957.

Inns Quay and O'Donovan Rossa Bridge from Merchant's Quay, Dublin.

1954

ORIGINAL TITLE: 'MAINLY DRIZZLE'.

EXHIBITED:
Photographic Society of Ireland, 1960.

Wellington Quay and Grattan Bridge from Liffey Bridge, Dublin.

C.1950

ORIGINAL TITLE: 'NOVEMBER EVENING'.

EXHIBITED:
Photographic Society of Ireland, 1952.
Salon na h-Éireann, 1952.
The Camera Club of Bermuda Photographic Exhibition, Hamilton, Bermuda, 1955.
VIII Salón Internacional de Fotografía, San Sebastian, 1955.
VIIᵉ Salon International d'Art Photographique, Photo-Club de Bordeaux, 1956.
An Óige Exhibition, An Tóstal, 1957.

Patrick Street, Dublin.
1956

Liffey Bridge (the Halfpenny Bridge), Dublin.

1956

EXHIBITED:
Photographic Society of Ireland, 1958.

Fatima Mansions, Rialto, Dublin.

1954

ORIGINAL TITLE: 'THAW'.

EXHIBITED:
Photographic Society of Ireland, 1957.

St. Augustine Street, Dublin.

1953

ORIGINAL TITLE: 'CONFERENCE'.

EXHIBITED:
Photographic Society of Ireland, 1955.
Internationale Foto und Verbandsausstellung, Berlin, 1955.
Salón Internacional de Fotografía de Vitoria, 1955.
VII Internationale Photo Ausstellung des Verbandes Österreichs der Amateurphotographervereine, 1956.
Salon na h-Éireann, 1956.

Dolphin House Flats, South Circular Road, Dublin.

1955

EXHIBITED:
An Óige Exhibition, An Tóstal, 1957.
Photographic Society of Ireland, 1957.

Middle Gardiner Street and Mountjoy Square, Dublin.
1956
ORIGINAL TITLE: 'DUBLIN TOWN IS FALLING DOWN'.

Áras Mhic Dhiarmada, (Busáras), Dublin.
1954

Bellamont Forest, Co. Cavan, entrance hall.
1961

Birr Castle, Co. Offaly.

1971

ORIGINAL TITLE: 'CHAIR PATTERN'.

EXHIBITED:
Photographic Society of Ireland, 1972.

Chapel, Maynooth College, Co. Kildare.
1952

Church of Christ the King, Turner's Cross, Cork.

1952

EXHIBITED:
Photographic Society of Ireland, 1953.
An Óige Exhibition, An Tóstal, 1957.

Kenure Park, Co. Dublin, entrance front.

1954

EXHIBITED:
Photographic Society of Ireland, 1956.
An Óige Exhibition, An Tóstal, 1957.

Springhill, Co. Derry, window.
1963

Leixlip Castle, Co. Kildare, bedroom.
1965

Dromana, Co. Waterford, staircase.
1962

Powerscourt, Co. Wicklow, entrance hall.
1967

Charleville, Co. Wicklow, entrance hall.

1964

EXHIBITED:
Photographic Society of Ireland, 1965.

Kilshannig, Co. Cork, entrance hall.
1959

Ballynegall, Co. Westmeath, main staircase.
1961

Ballynegall, Co. Westmeath, drawing room.
1961

Furness, Co. Kildare, staircase hall.
1968

Stradbally Hall, Co. Laois, dining room.
1959

Carton, Co. Kildare, saloon.
1962

Castletown, Co. Kildare, view of entrance hall from main staircase.
1961

Moore Abbey, Co. Kildare, hall.
1962

Newberry Hall, Co. Kildare, entrance hall.
1959

Castlemartin, Co. Kildare, staircase hall.
1985

Vernon Mount, Co. Cork, main staircase.
1965

Mount Juliet, Co. Kilkenny, main staircase.
1967

Lyons, Co. Kildare, view from large drawing room to small drawing room.
1961

Unidentified coastal house, Co. Antrim.

1955

EXHIBITED:
Photographic Society of Ireland, 1960.

Cheering President Kennedy?, location unknown.

1963

ORIGINAL TITLE: 'LOOK! BRIAN BORU'.

EXHIBITED:
International Cork Photographic Exhibition, 1966.

Cottages, The Claddagh, Galway.

1952

ORIGINAL TITLE: 'IN OLD GALWAY'.

Thomas McNamara, guide to Killone Abbey, Co. Clare.

1952

EXHIBITED:
Photographic Society of Ireland, 1953.
An Óige Exhibition, An Tóstal, 1957.

Mahmoud Khamis, guide to the Hashemite Kingdom of Jordan.
1955

Liam Bourke, guide to the power station at Ardnacrusha, Co. Clare.
1952

Architectural photography

AN ILLUSTRATED TALK BY HUGH DORAN

Not only did Hugh Doran regularly contribute architectural photographs to the Photographic Society of Ireland (PSI) and other exhibitions, he also gave illustrated talks on the subject of architectural photography. Using examples of photographs he had taken himself, he covered such topics as composition and framing, lens selection, exposure and printing. Reproduced here are the illustrative images for one of these lectures, originally delivered by Hugh in the mid-1970s, with extracts from the original speaking notes.

Hugh Doran (1926-2004)

I began my hobby with a cardboard box camera in 1945. Then I acquired a Zeiss Baby Ikonta which took 16 shots on 127 film. It had a 4.5 Novar lens and a three speed shutter - 1/25, 1/50, 1/75 of a second. I made an enlarger using the lens from the camera and I enjoyed myself for a few years until I joined the PSI (Photographic Society of Ireland) in 1949 and bought a 6 x 9 Ensign Selfix with a 3.8 Ross Xpres lens. This is probably the sharpest lens I have ever owned. Then I had Rolleiflexes until 1959 when I was asked by Desmond Guinness to shoot a number of curved wing houses for an exhibition he was mounting.

Taking pictures for pleasure [is] one thing, shooting an assignment is another and I knew that my Rollei would not cope with the angles that Desmond wanted. So regretfully I had to trade in my Rollei for a 6 x 9 Linhof with wide angle [and] normal lenses and a Rollfilm back. I feel that I got better pictures with the Rolleis but I sold a lot of shots from the Linhof so that after only one year with the new camera I could afford to buy another Rollei and later I bought a Contax outfit which enabled me to shoot architectural colour slides.

So tonight I will show you some of the pictures I made with Rolleiflex cameras followed by Linhof pictures.

King's Inns, Henrietta Street, Dublin, entrance hall.

A sturdy tripod is recommended for architectural photography. Years ago wits said 'the smaller the camera the bigger the stand'. PSI outing... Film slows up on prolonged exposure. For this shot the exposure was so long that [I] got a cramp!

St. Patrick's Cathedral (RC), Armagh, pulpit.

'Lead kindly light'. Another PSI outing. For [this picture] the beauty is in the light on the stairs and balusters.

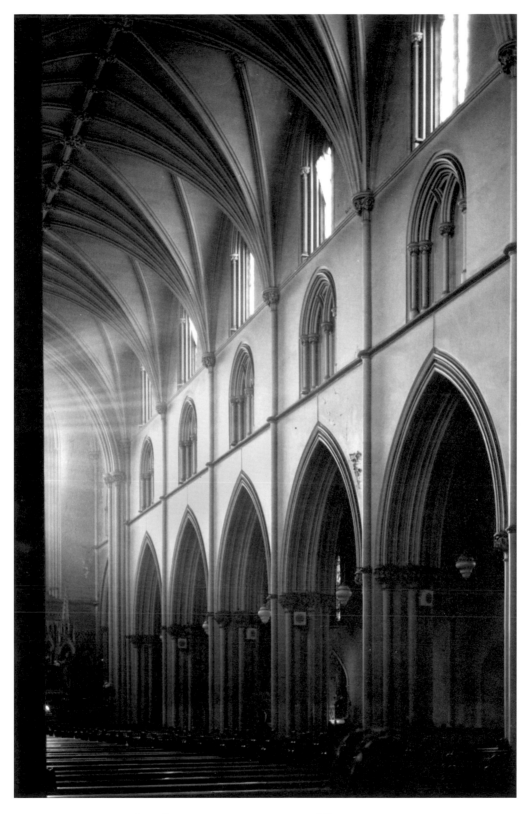

St. James's Church (RC), James's Street, Dublin.

Here I feel the sunbeams do give some atmosphere to the shot. I had shot this church to illustrate a lecture by a friend on the architect Patrick Byrne and I thought that some winter sun would make a picture of the rather drab interior. So I kept the church under observation and eventually, on a Saturday morning in January, I shot this picture.

Ely House, Ely Place, Dublin, staircase.

This is now the headquarters of the Knights of St. Columbanus and it has this famous staircase with its statue of Hercules... I feel that the sunlight helps the picture, though the window is overexposed and requires printing-in during enlarging. If possible the picture and magazine rack and the statue in the background should be removed.

Belvedere College, Great Denmark Street, Dublin, staircase.

In the absence of a state scheme for the preservation of buildings of outstanding architectural merit, we should thank our lucky stars that we [have] religious orders who will keep them in first class order. I was able to use a doorcase to block out a window that would have been too much of a highlight if it had been included. Unfortunately I was not able to get rid of the lampshade.

Belvedere College, Great Denmark Street, Dublin, staircase detail.

'Some of the 18th century ironwork is very fine. Be careful to expose for the metal which is much darker than its surroundings. Note the gentle rise in the stairs.

Chapel Royal, Dublin Castle, staircase.

An early 19th century stairs that looks much smaller in reality. The wide angle exaggerates. Once again you must balance your exposure to give reasonable detail in the dark areas. Some areas require shading during printing.

St. Audoen's Church (RC), High Street, Dublin.

This church was also designed by Patrick Byrne whom we last met in James's Street.
Maurice Craig thinks that this is Byrne's masterpiece. When you tilt the camera when
using the wide angle lens make sure that the centre line of both camera and subject are
in line. If they are not you will get distortion. Luckily for me the church had been
recently decorated. Some printing-in required on left of picture.

20 Dominick Street Lower, Dublin, ceiling detail.

This house was once the home of Robert West, a famous 18th century stuccadore. Some of the plaster birds stand out 15 inches from the wall. Here I felt that the available light did not show the figures well enough, so I lit the corner with two photo floods which gave stronger modelling. Once again the centre line must be straight.

Powerscourt, Co. Wicklow, ceiling.

The house was burnt in October 1974 and I was the last photographer to shoot the interior. The print required some burning in.

Mellerstain House, Berwickshire, Scotland, ceiling.

These next two shots require the camera back to be parallel to the ceiling and it can be difficult as you try to frame the picture while the tripod gets in your way.

St. George's Church, Hardwicke Place, Dublin, ceiling detail.

Francis Johnston was the architect. It had been recently decorated when I shot it.

St. Patrick's Cathedral (RC), Armagh, gates.

Another PSI outing shot. I set up the Linhof, opened the shutter at time and got one of the members who had an electronic flash to fire it a few times from the other side.

Mountjoy Square, Dublin.

This shot is impossible today with parked cars. For this shot I had to tilt the camera and correct the verticals during enlarging.

Castle Coole, Co. Fermanagh, drawing room.

A Wyatt house, the seat of the Earls of Belmore, now in the care of the Northern Ireland National Trust... Windows are included but they can be printed in during enlarging.

Russborough, Co. Wicklow, entrance hall.

*Residence of Sir Alfred Beit who bought it in 1951. It is said that he discarded every-
thing in the mansion except for one table and that it took a year to hang all Sir Alfred's
collection of pictures. As the lighting is very uneven quite a bit of shading is necessary.*

Arcade, Belgrade, Serbia.

It isn't often that we have pictures presented to us on a plate, as it were, but I felt that this was such an occasion. Wide angle lens, camera on tripod and a reasonable wait until a suitable figure appeared. I was late for lunch but it was worth it. In a shot like this over development of the negative must be avoided like the plague.

Palazzo dello Sport, Rome, Italy.

By Pier Luigi Nervi. A good exercise in exposing a negative and a good test of your printing ability.

Doge's Palace, Venice, Italy, ceiling detail.

Another directly overhead shot that required manipulating at the printing stage to yield a good print.

Kenwood House, London, England, ceiling.

Robert Adam's finest library. One is allowed to shoot and the place is heated, so that it is ideal for winter photography.

Index of architectural illustrations